LILLENAS®

DRAMA

EVE'S

DAUGHTERS

Modern Monologues for Women

by

Gail Blanton

Lillenas PUBLISHING COMPANY

KANSAS CITY, MO 64141

Dedication

To my daughter, Lisa Blanton Yauilla. Despite my bumbling, inexperienced, er—uh—creative, mothering, she was a delightful child and has become a godly, compassionate woman; a sweet and attentive mother; a wonderful and understanding friend to me; a source of fun, joy, and pride.

Contents

Introduction

Like our distant mother, Eve, we women also long to walk and talk with God in the cool quietness of some beautiful place, to discover His perfect path for our lives. It is not easy among the consequences of the sinful nature we inherited. We have so many desires—some noble, some not. There are so many distractions, such subtle deceptions, such stark disappointments. Whether they spring from our wrong choices or from no fault of our own, our dilemmas often prove we are our first mother's descendants: Eve's daughters all. Like her, we find ourselves in hiding and less than honest with the very God who would understand and guide us, in hiding and less than honest with other Christians who could be a help to us. Perhaps we feel that if we would only get our act together, God would bless us like He does that wonder-woman Christian in our church.

For those who have lived with any of the situations in this book, the general ones or the more intimate ones, these monologues are meant to give public voice to some of the feelings that you might not be comfortable sharing. For those who have not experienced any of these problems, I hope hearing the pieces will serve as a reminder that we never know what others are dealing with privately or why they may act as they do. Nor do we know when we may confront the same problem.

Many of these scripts were written intentionally to expose from a woman's point of view very personal, sensitive issues that are too often hushed up. Why these subjects? They are certainly not as much fun. The answers are many: because of the hurt and the questioning in the voices that, over the years, have chosen to confide in me. Because they think there are few people who have their type of problem. Because they suppose that most people in their church family live relatively carefree lives and so would be aghast at their stories. Because we are all reluctant to admit our failures and doubts, even though they would make others feel freer to share with us. Because it is easier to wear a mask of superior "Life is always wonderful" Christianity than to become accountable or require others to be. Because sometimes church has been the least comfortable place to bare our deepest feelings. Because all of us need to learn more about how to "Bear one another's burdens, and thus fulfill the law of Christ" (Galatians 6:2, RSV).

Even when we don't know all the answers or can't provide immediate solutions, we can listen well enough to understand the problem. We can provide a safe atmosphere by being open and honest ourselves. We can refuse to participate in gossip. We can care, cry, support materially or physically, and refuse to judge. We can hug. We can love. We can remember grace and offer it. We can "do to others what you would have them do to you" (Matthew 7:12, NASB). We can be true daughters of the beautiful, fortunate Eve, who was God's own precious creation, who received favor in the first promise of our coming Savior as Restorer of godly relationships.

Some of the monologues herein do not come to a resolution; indeed, the issues are too great to even pretend they might be resolved in a five- or six-minute presentation. For that reason, these particular scripts should be followed by a sermon, Bible study, support group, experienced counselor, or qualified consultant addressing the topic from a godly perspective. We want to leave the audience with hope, not despair. These scripts include "Alone in the Crowd," "Family Secrets," "Chained."

Of course, the other scripts may benefit from follow-up also, but it is not necessary.

As mentioned above, we do need fun, so a couple of the scripts are lighter fare—humor but with a message.

Finally, I have included a poetic piece in the hope that it will please some tiny part of your feminine desire for beauty.

To Him who is perfect in beauty and calls us to grow in the beauty of holiness, all praise and glory.

Oh My Joyce!

Scripture Allusion: Exodus 20:7; Isaiah 42:8; Romans 14:19

Topic: A woman gains new understanding of taking God's name in vain.

Cast:
> JOYCE

Scene: A place she is comfortable—home, tidying up; or office, arranging her desk

Props:
> Furniture and items to suggest a room at home or an office

Approximate Playing Time: 2 minutes

(We catch JOYCE *in the middle of a conversation with an unseen friend. For stage business, she may tidy the room or arrange her desk.)*

JOYCE: You know, I've never been one of those people who thought profanity was a big deal. I was practically weaned on it, as they say. In fact, my folks used four-letter words just like ordinary words. Once I started school, it didn't take me long to learn that they were not considered ordinary vocabulary to the teachers. Apparently my parents' idea of raising a child was scandalous. Or, as my parents preferred to call it, enlightened. Anyway, I soon became a split personality as far as my speech. I could talk one way at school, another at home. So, as an adult, it wasn't a big stretch when I became a Christian to discover I can talk one way at church, another at home.

> Sure, I learned about the commandment not to take God's name in vain, and some of the words used God's name, but I've never felt any guilt about it. It's just a manner of speaking. Not in an angry, swearing way—just casually, like when something shocks me or when I see something wonderful. I mean, it's pretty commonplace to hear it all the time. Oh my this, and oh my that. I don't mean any disrespect at all. God knows how much I love Him, how much I appreciate all He's done for me. When I call His name that way, I don't mean it literally. It's just an old habit.

> Speaking of habits, I guess you know I'm now in my second marriage. My husband, Reggie, and I have worked through most of our adjustments. One thing still bothers me though. If someone wants to do something in a hurry, he'll say, "OK, just do the Joyce version then!" See, Reggie thinks I cut corners on things sometimes. I don't—it's just that he's such a perfectionist. He doesn't say it in a mean way. It's more like he's teasing, but I still don't like it. He says things like, "Now that's a Joyce car wash for you." I don't appreciate being used as an adjective.

> Then yesterday, he was in a big way of talking and he called me by his

first wife's name, then mine. Real quick, like "Marie—Joyce . . . " It really got away with him. Now, I know perfectly well my husband loves me very much. I also know he called me Marie simply out of an old habit. But frankly, even though I didn't show it, it still hurt.

So, I was thinking this morning about why I was so upset, and I realized that the real me is somehow connected to my name. And it hurts when people use it in the wrong way, even if they mean no harm. "The fact is," I had to admit, "it really matters to me how someone uses my name."

And God said to me, "Bingo."

That's What I Want

Scripture Allusion: Isaiah 30:18; Ephesians 5:28; Revelation 2:4

Topic: God longs for a loving relationship as much as humans do.

Cast:
> MARGIE—a hairstylist
> CLIENT—woman who never speaks; or, she may be imaginary and the styling pantomimed

Scene: A hairstyling salon

Props:
> A hairstyling chair
> If Client is real—brush, comb, rollers, and other hairstyling tools, including a drape
> A small table

Approximate Playing Time: 3 minutes

(Lights up on a chair in which CLIENT *sits. She is covered with a drape.* MARGIE *stands, rolling, cutting, or styling her hair throughout the monologue. Her styling tools are on a small table to one side.)*

MARGIE: Well, honey, I don't blame you for wanting a new hairstyle. We just get tired of the same old thing every day, don't we? I've tried 8 or 10 myself in the last year—about three different colors. I don't know if any of it has done any good though. I just want to look the best I can, don't you? I just keep on trying, thinking the next thing will bring out the real me, you know?

> I tried that platinum blonde one time. I don't know, I thought it was kinda glamorous or something. Honey, my mother did not like *that.* Not that she likes anything I do. She told me it looked—well, she told me what it looked like. I just wanted to do something a little daring for my anniversary trip. Where was the harm? It made me feel romantic until she spoiled it all with that comment. Didn't even ask me how I liked it before she let loose.

> And then my husband's wanting to know what's wrong. I know better, but I finally tell him anyway. And he's telling me that I *always* let her do that and telling me what I should say back. Always trying to fix things for me, but he doesn't even want to listen to the story of what the real problem is.

> Just like my daddy, honey. He would fix any of my toys, anything in the house, anything at the church, but he didn't even know when my birthday was or that I was scared of monsters hiding underneath my bed, even after I was a teenager.

Anyway, I think if I fix myself up a little more for my husband, you know, get a new look that sort of excites him, maybe he'll pay more attention to me and we can talk more. Maybe it's just a man thing, but sometimes I wonder if he even wants to know me any better—like it might require something he doesn't want to do.

Don't get me wrong, honey. We get along fine for the most part. But more and more I feel like there's something we've lost—or maybe we never even found. It just seems like something's missing and I started feeling sad most of the time without really knowing why.

But this is the most amazing thing. It's hard to believe, but I know you go to church and all, so I can tell you. I couldn't let it get out to the rest of the people in the shop. Honey, they would think I had bleached my brain. I got to feeling so bad Tuesday night. I had an awful day at work, I got some bad news on the telephone that day too, and I just couldn't wait to get home and do nothing—maybe get some sympathy. But everybody there was stressed out with their own stuff and expecting something from me.

After they were in bed, I just got down on my knees and cried and tried to talk to God. You know I'm not a religious person, but I figured nobody else would listen, what did I have to lose? You know what? He said something back. I mean, I didn't hear it out loud, but it was so real I almost freaked out. When I started out I was just having a pity party, saying things like, "I know my family must care about me, but I wish they would tell me or show me that more often. I wish they would remember that I have feelings too and that they really hurt me sometimes; that I just wish somebody would take the time to know me better, to find out what would really please me. Somebody who thinks I'm beautiful and exciting. I just want somebody to really, truly love me with a passion." And then, honey, can you believe it, God said, "So do I. That's what I want for myself too."

I can't stop thinking about it. It's got me all—I don't know—discombobulated or something. I just have never thought about it that way. Have you?

Service du Jour

Scripture Allusion: Psalm 84:10-11; Galatians 5:13

Topic: Are we more concerned with serving others or making sure we are served in the manner we prefer?

Cast:
> MANDY—a "server" for a worship service paralleling a server in a restaurant

Scene: Your worship service

Props:
> Printed order of worship
> Wristwatch

Approximate Playing Time: 2-3 minutes

(Preferably this sketch opens the worship service. MANDY directs her opening lines toward the back, as if the main part of the sanctuary is empty with a large crowd standing in the back, waiting to be seated.)

MANDY: Excuse me, is everyone inside back there? Everyone who was on the waiting list? Everyone whose little palm-held reservation thingie lit up? The little thing that flashed and *(pounce on the pronunciation of "buzzed" as if it is an attack)* buzzed and scared the living daylights out of you? OK then. Julio, tell the others outside their wait will be one hour. *([Insert the time your service is supposed to last.] Clears throat.)* More or less.

Good morning, ladies and gentlemen. My name is Mandy and I'll be your server today. Now, would you prefer *(indicates opposite sides of the room)* Clapping or Nonclapping section? And would you prefer Shaking or Nonshaking? Please be aware that if you sit in the Nonclapping section, then you cannot shake hands. So, if you care to shake hands, you must sit in the Clapping Section. I'm sorry for any inconvenience, but that is the new Code. We can't discriminate with our hands, now can we? What's that? No, I'm sorry, if you're undecided, you'll have to exit now. We seat those who are undecided in the middle of the road.

All right, you may take your seats. Just follow the usher of your choice: Fred, in the orange coat, plaid pants, and polka dot tie; Matt in all black with the Tazmanian Devil tie—go get 'em, Taz! or Butch in the chartreuse coat, yellow tie, and gray gym shorts. He works with the youth.

As advertised, for those of you who are the first to sit right down front, we are passing out these free *(holds one up)* automatic alarm watches. Now these *are* preset to alarm at 12:00, *[substitute the time your service should end]* 12:02, 04, 06, 08, and so forth. If we have not finished serving you when the last one goes off, you get a free personalized sermon delivered right to your door.

Now, could I get your drink order? *(Pretends to be storing the orders in her mind as she makes appropriate comments)* OK. All right. Uh-huh, got that. O-O-O-OK *(Rattles them off rapidly, mumbling almost to herself various drinks)* Tea, coffee, water, decaf, Coke *[etc.]*. *(Quickly)* Sorry, we only have grape juice and water.

Would you like to hear about our specials today? We have a prime solo. That is a filet of song laid on a bed of soft piano music, seasoned with tone and modulation, and brought to you on a red-hot microphone. We also have a theme interpretation simmered in dramatic action, seasoned with laughter, and that comes with applause on the side.

While you're deciding, could I bring you an appetizer? We have a prelude, a call to worship, a welcome, and a prayer. Or I can bring a sample section of each for everyone to share.

While you're deciding, let me give you your choices for music. We offer contemporary, classical, hymns, praise band, anthems, easy listening, gospel, Christian rock, and oldies.

While you're deciding, I'll tell you that our breads today are Matthew 4:4 and John 6:35. *[Or substitute the scriptures you will be using that day.]* Our normal gratuity is 10 percent minimum, plus added amounts according to the quality of your blessings. Our pastor du jour is *[name of pastor]* and our sermon du jour is "Are You Serving or Being Served?" We hope you'll enjoy our menu, but if not, we trust you'll eat heartily anyway.

Well, I'll give you a few minutes to decide, and someone will be here in a moment with your drinks.

(You may follow immediately after she exits with the reading of Isaiah 55:1-3a, Jeremiah 6:35, one of the scriptures mentioned above, or with special music about living bread or living water.)

Family Secrets

Scripture Allusion: Psalm 18:46-48; Ephesians 5:28-33

Topic: A church member is confronted by a friend in like circumstances planning to expose their Christian husbands' physical abuse.

Cast:
> TESS—an abused wife

Scene: Her home

Props:
> Furniture to suggest home
> Large stuffed animal (well-worn, torn in places, perhaps with an ear hanging half off)

Approximate Playing Time: 5 minutes

(TESS talks to a friend, Julie, unseen by the audience. During entire monologue, she fingers, pats, hugs, etc., a large stuffed animal that has seen better days. Perhaps she tries to pull the torn places together. She is unaware that she makes any of these actions.)

TESS: No, no Julie. I can't tell anybody. Can't ever tell. What in the world would people say? Everybody thinks we're the perfect couple. Can you imagine the gossip? Assuming they even believed it, which I doubt they would. No, no hope of that. They think Ben's a saint. The men would say I must do something to deserve it. Maybe I do. Maybe if I could just do things the way he wants me to. But that seems to change depending on his mood. What bothers me the most, I think, is that it's always such a shock. Things will be rolling along so smoothly and we'll be getting along so well. I begin to think that I can forget what he's done, that he's really changed. I'm so happy. Then, wham! I'm blind-sided. I'm saying, "What? What did I do?" Some of the most petty things can set him off. He can't control himself, but he wants to control me. If he even knew I was talking to you about this he would make me regret it.

I wish you had just kept pretending you didn't know. Absolutely not, Julie. I don't want you to do anything about it. It will just make him treat me worse. Even if he didn't, I'm just not able to deal with the fallout. If anybody did believe me, I'd just be handed that stuff about being a submissive wife. I'd be so embarrassed. And the children—oh, my goodness—can you imagine? Besides, scripture says, "Love . . . bears all things, believes all things, hopes all things, endures all things." No, I don't want to be a doormat, but I don't see that I have much choice— *(getting huffy)* God doesn't expect me to live with that? Oh yeah? Well, how would you know? How would you know anything in the world about it?

(Stunned pause) What? No. Not you too. No, stop. I don't want to hear this. I've always admired Preston so much. He's chairman of the deacons, for heaven's sake. You two have taught me half of what I know about the Bible. Why couldn't you just let me go on believing? Pornography? No, thank God, as far as I know Ben was never into that.

I know your heart is broken. You must feel so betrayed. I'm so sorry, Julie. I have no consolation, except now we can cry our secret tears together.

You're going to report him? To whom? I don't think you want to do that, Julie. Aren't you terrified? You're gonna scandalize the whole church. It's your word against his. You're gonna make him furious! Proof? You put it in a safe place, I hope. And I hope you have a safe place to go too because he's gonna be stalking you. He's gonna make you so sorry you'll wish you had kept your mouth shut. Please, just let it go.

Why are you so determined now, after all these years? Well, of course it would be worth it if you encouraged some other woman to stand up for her dignity and stop taking the abuse. But do you really think our speaking out is going to change anything at all? Yeah, I know there's strength in numbers, but even if I decided to help you, 2 wouldn't be many in a church of 2,000. *(Pause)* You have at least 2 others. *(Puts hands over her own ears)* No. No, don't tell me. The church is God's family. How can all this be happening in God's family? *(Uncovers her ears)* What do you mean, a man? His wife abuses him? You mean she puts him down all the time? Hitting and scratching?

(Puts her head in her hands) God in heaven, how many more? I thought I was the only one. So . . . OK . . . maybe we could go to a support group or something. What am I saying? If Ben found out, I'd be dead meat, maybe literally. I guess you're right. If you don't go public, you may not know how many victims there are.

Victim—oh my—I don't think that's what I am. I mean, I know Ben's anger is coming from some deep hurt in his past, and he's a pretty good guy for the most part. After all, we all have our faults. Do we have any right to expose someone else?

Well, don't yell at me. Isn't that what we've always seen in a church? It's always "Look the other way." "Live and let live." Smile and be holy. But like you say, maybe that *is* part of the problem.

No, I can't say I'm angry about it. There's so much anger at home that I don't want to add mine to it. Mostly I feel nothing—just numb. And I don't think I can deal with a church full of anger. Would anybody forgive us? Or forgive them? What terms would they have to meet before we forgive them? Would we have to leave our husbands? Leave the church? What about the young people who look up to us? This is way too much to try to digest all at once. I'll just have to think about it, Julie, and get back to you.

But don't count on me. Because I think my situation is different from those you're talking about. It's not so bad most of the time. Ben doesn't mean to hurt me, it just sort of happens before he knows it, he says. He's really been doing better lately. If you only knew the stress he's under at work, you'd wonder how he copes at all.

Actually, I should keep the kids under better control so he can have some peace and quiet at home. Plus, I surely haven't kept myself up like I should have, to look good for him. So, I've sorta resolved to try a little harder and then I think things will work themselves out. Ben makes us a good living, doesn't drink or run around. He's honest, and he loves the Lord. I could do a lot worse. Maybe I—uh—gave you the wrong impression. It's really not all that serious. Nothing we can't work out. But I will pray for you and those who are in real trouble, that you'll know what to do about it. Just be careful.

Prissy Kate

Scripture Allusion: Leviticus 19:32; Isaiah 46:4

Topic: A woman and her aging mother reverse roles.

Cast:
> KATE—age 50 to 60

Scene: Her home

Props:
> Shoebox holding a pair of ladies' high heel shoes

Approximate Playing Time: 6 minutes

KATE *(takes one or both shoes out of the box; looks at them fondly, chuckling):* I remember when I was a little girl and loved to play dress-up. The shinier, the silkier, the lacier, *(twirls around)* the twirlier, the more I adored it. Picture hats, velvet cloches, hats with fishnet veils that covered my face. Jewelry and handbags and—oh my—elbow-length gloves like a movie star.

All of those things could be pinned up or tied up with a sash or adjusted somehow to my size. But not the shoes. No matter how much paper I crammed in the toes, I could never master the art of looking elegant while clomping around in my mother's high heels. I could walk in them really well—goodness knows, I practiced enough—it was just that they really cramped my image of myself. Head to ankles, I was the breathtaking beauty of Broadway. From there on down it was the clunking clodhopper. I longed with all my little prissy heart for a pair of real high heels that fit me. You know the dress-up shoes they sell now that fit little girls, the plastic ones? This was way before that. Shoot, it was probably before plastic. So it seemed my style was doomed to clompiness.

Then one beautiful day our family moved. After I got bored with running in and out and slamming the doors of our new house, I wandered out and spied a big box at the curb. I figured it was left by the former tenants. I had pulled out about three-quarters of the stuff when I thought I spotted something made of brown lizard skin. Ooooo, fancy. What was it? My mouth dropped open in disbelief. I dived in headfirst, spitting out a wayward mothball and turning the whole thing over. It was a pair of dress shoes with skinny high heels, not too scuffed up, and just my size. I found out later that a little person had lived there, midgets we called them back then. I tell you, I was ecstatic before I even knew what ecstatic meant!

Mama said I could have them, but she didn't have time to hunt my dress-up box. So we draped a curtain around me and I put on my wonderful shoes. It was a less than graceful debut. I hadn't realized Mama's larger shoes and wider heels had much more area to balance on. I wobbled. I weaved. I waved my arms to keep my balance. When I finally thought I had it, I started my grand walk across the room. But after a couple of proud steps I was wavering again. Ooops. Steady. Ooops. Mama's saying, "Be careful. Slow down." Then she can't help herself, she's snickering and walking behind me with both arms out until one giant wobble, and we both fall on the floor in a heap. After Mama found out I wasn't hurt, we lay back on the floor and laughed and laughed. We laughed till we cried. Before too long I got the knack of it and, considering all my finery, I'm not surprised I got the nickname Prissy Kate.

Mama. She's always understood me better than anyone as far as what my deepest heart of hearts really wants. And she's always either helped me get it or encouraged me to get it or rejoiced when I got it. Always supported me even when others didn't get the point of what I was doing. Nothing I do is so silly that she can't be proud of me. So it was only natural that I asked her to come live with us when she got sick.

I have to admit, it's been a real adjustment. It hasn't been easy, even as much as we love each other. But in other ways, it's been wonderful spending more time with her, trying to absorb some of her wisdom and patience while I can. These are precious days. She's still full of spunk, even though there are lots of days when she's too weak to do much of anything. Then there are periods of time when she feels pretty good and we can do things together. Then she likes to get all fixed up. It's like old times, except that her dress is more practical now.

Last night we gave her a birthday party at a fancy restaurant. She's been so excited all week. Yesterday afternoon she yelled, "Prissy Kate, come look at this." She had on a rose-colored silk suit, pearl jewelry, stars in her eyes, and cream high heels on her feet. She looked beautiful.

"Mama, I don't know about those shoes."

"I think they look fantastic," she said and twirled around. I told her they looked wonderful but I wasn't sure they were sensible. "Who wants to be sensible?" she asked.

"Safe, then," I answered.

"Don't be ridiculous. I've worn these for years," she said and took off toward the full-length mirror. She was so pleased with herself that I couldn't help but grin. But her ankles just weren't up to it. I tried to keep her from falling, but we both fell in a heap on the carpet. Thank heavens she wasn't hurt. She slowly took off the shoes, handed them to me, and told me to put them in the trash at the curb. "Maybe some little girl can play with them," she said. She looked at me with wide, wistful eyes and stated simply, "I just wanted to be glamorous for my birthday."

I threw my arms around her and we cried and cried. We lay back on the floor and cried. Suddenly she sat up and yelled, "For crying out loud!" grabbed one of the shoes and threw it against the wall. Then she got tickled, so I got tickled too. I threw the other shoe against the wall and we lay back on the carpet and laughed and laughed. Mama and me, kicking up our heels like always.

Found: God's Will

Scripture Allusion: Daniel 4:35; Matthew 10:38-39; James 4:14-15

Topic: God's will for our lives is moving and active, and we cannot ascertain it once for all time.

Cast:
> WOMAN (or teenager)—Lively, high-spirited. She says, "I mean" as a habit of her character. This is not redundancy in the text.

Scene: Bare stage

Props: A large box

Approximate Playing Time: 2 minutes

(Speaking directly to audience from extreme DS)

WOMAN: Pssssst! *(Motions audience to come closer)* Have you been searching for God's Will? I knew it. I just knew it. So have I. I mean, looking everywhere. Can you believe how hard it is to find? I mean, sometimes I feel like I've spent my whole life looking for God's Will. I mean, why should it be so difficult? How many places can it be hiding, right? I'm so glad you've been looking for a long time too because—listen to this—oh, I'm so excited—just listen to this: I've found it! I have actually found it. Isn't that exciting? I mean, we don't have to look anymore. Come on, I'll show you!

There it is—right there. Isn't it wonderful? God's Will right there in a box. I still can't quite believe it. God's Will in a container where it can be seen and measured and examined and—well—contained. I mean, it's not much good to anybody if it was going to remain *(finger motions)* out there somewhere all spooky and mysterious. At last I've got it confined under such conditions that I can watch it and calculate it and figure out how to manage it.

(Unseen person starts to open the box.) Watch it! No, no! We don't want to open it yet. It's going to be great just to keep it there for, oh, I'd say several years, just to contemplate the fact that we've got God's Will locked up in our own little box. It is unbelievable. I mean, as long as it's here, I doubt if anyone else will be able to find it. *(Becomes childishly selfish)* We could watch them trying, just like we've always tried to find it, and give them advice: "You're warm . . . warmer. Hot! Literally burning up! Cold! Error! Error!"

I mean, there's no hurry, right? After all, we have found it, and that is a major accomplishment. Hmmm? Well, I guess we could take a tiny peek if you really want to. But what if it escaped through a crack? I mean, before we had time to decide what to do with it? We might never find it again. Worse, what if we open it and don't like what we see? I mean,

20

there's no guarantee, right? I mean, what if it's not very pleasant? What if it's downright ugly? Or dangerous? We don't have any way of knowing. I mean, it could even be deadly. I don't know about you, but I don't want to die—not me, myself or I. Why should that be necessary? I mean, how rigid can you get?

No, I'm just going to do what I'm supposed to and let God's Will be done . . . right there in that little box. And there will always be such peace in my heart just knowing: I searched for God's Will, and I found it!

Six Flags over Church

Scripture Allusion: Psalm 84:1-2, 10; Psalm 100:4; Psalm 111:1

Topic: A family goes to as much trouble to attend church as they would to attend an amusement park.

Cast:
MOTHER

Scene:
1. In the family car
2. In the parking lot of the church
3. Inside the church

Props: Everything is mimed

Approximate Playing Time: 4 minutes

MOTHER (*pantomimes driving car. Kids are in the car with her, unseen by the audience. Light turn red, slams on brakes*): Rats! If that guy would let me in that lane . . . Try to get his attention, kids. (*Motions, "Can I get over there ahead of you?" He says no; she gestures in disgust.*) Yeah, same to you, buddy. Come on, light, turn; turn! Anytime . . . Yes! (*Floorboards it and swerves in front of him; looking back*) Got in anyway, pagan!

All right, kids, just settle down now. We're almost there—top of this next hill, then—awww—look at the lines. Such a cloudy day, I thought maybe the crowd would be off. Well, it's not my fault we didn't leave earlier. I wasn't on the phone begging all my friends to go with me. Yes, well, when they refused, you could have refrained from telling them where they might go. Your *deacon* told you to say that? Who does he think he is? Yes, I know he's *[name of deacon or elder or staff member, etc.]*, but he shouldn't—never mind. Just wait till I see him!

Just shut up, Kelly; you're no better. Whining around because Steven just broke up with you and he might be here today. As if you would ever see him in this crowd. He's singing a solo? Here? But he sings through his nose! Uh—I said, the things that he knows! All those temporary songs. Yes, of course, contemporary. Well, you can stay outside till he finishes and then come in and find us. We'll try to sit in Section 8 as usual.

(*Looks to left*) No, you can't get over here. No, no way. People with these expensive cars! Always think they own the road. No! Quit trying to edge over. (*Rolls window down*) OK mister, we see your front end and we don't care to see anything else! Oh yeah? Well, we know of this place that rhymes with Mercedes! (*Pause for audience to get the connection*) Heathen! (*Turns corner*) OK, kids, which gate, A, B, C, or D? Which line looks shorter? Hurry! C it is. (*Shows pass*) Season membership. Thank you. (*Drives in; to parking attendant*) No, I don't want to go in that row. Quit motioning me in there! Young man, do you realize that I help pay your salary? Now move over and let me in that next row. Thank you. *(Rolls window back up)*

(Drives and parks) Ah, good. Not too far from the entrance on this end. *(Getting out)* OK, kids, let's move it—make sure we get in. Somebody is going to bang my doors up; I just know it. Why do they make these parking spaces so little? Squeeze in more people. Well, I guess that just proves it's good. There wouldn't be a crowd unless it was good.

Uh-oh, step it up, kids. Let's get ahead of the crowd coming off that bus. *(Passing around several people)* Good morning. How are you today? *(Back to kids)* They won't let this many people in. Move in here, close in; squeeze right up there. Now, if we get separated, we all know where to meet, right? They're opening the doors; here we go. *(Acts as if moving in a mob, jostling people, pushing, etc.)* Excuse me; pardon me; sorry. Uh, we're all together—let them in, please. Whew! Made it.

(To someone behind) Yeah, it's too bad. You almost got in. You know, you really should come on a day during the week. It's much less crowded then. *(Back to kids)* OK, spread out—one in each line—and we'll make it to the front of the lobby together. Does everybody have their money? *(Almost fighting with several people)* No, I believe *I* was here first. *(Looking beside her)* Hey! Don't you try to get in front of him just because he's little. Watch out over there, Kelly; people will try to break in line. *(Counting heads in each line, speaks to person in front of her)* Excuse me, would you mind if I go in front of you so I'll be even with my kids and we can sit together? Thank you; that's really sweet of you. I don't think I've ever seen you here before. First time? Well, you'll love it. Everybody does, obviously. Well, here we are. Hope to see you again. Let's go, kids.

(Hand in air, calling) Program! Program! *(She gets one)* Let's see what's on the schedule today. Oh wonderful! I just love the hymns we're singing. It really doesn't matter, though. Everything is always good. Look how excited everybody is just because they actually got in. When so many people want to come to God's house that we run out of room, that's what I call a thrill! You gotta fight the crowds for anything worthwhile, and church— why it's worth whatever you gotta do to get here. You hear wonderful things in this place that you just don't hear anywhere else. I'm glad the word is getting out. Let's get to our seats. We don't want to miss anything God has to show us. Hurry up; sit down—it's show time!

Mary Martha

Scripture Allusion: Luke 10:38-42

Topic: Personal time with God is more important than doing other important things.

Cast:
MARY—a homemaker and mother

Scene: Patio (DS); kitchen (US)

Props:
Portable telephone
All others are mimed

Approximate Playing Time: 4 minutes

(Lights up on MARY *with portable phone held between her shoulder and ear, briskly pantomiming various household chores US.)*

MARY: Well, Betty, I don't know if Elsie is the best one to represent us or not. Well, if you can't get anyone else, I suppose, but she does say some of the most ridiculous things sometimes. Well . . . for instance, yesterday in Sunday School when they told us to think about whether we are a Martha-type or Mary-type, I said, "Oh, I'm Mary!" I was just making an obvious joke about my name; but she said that I might be named Mary, but I was more like Martha. Can you believe that? All my friends know I'm more interested in the spiritual side of things. Everyone knows I write all those poems, and it takes a contemplative person to do that. And those deep thoughts everybody says I have—I wonder if she thinks I get them out of a cookbook. Well, you know, like the one I had the other day in the mall about the elevator, escalator, and fire escape being like three different kinds of spiritual growth? Uh-huh, see, I'm definitely a Mary. Not like Martha—she was just too concerned with physical things. Listen, I've got a lot to do today; I'd better run. OK, 'bye.

(Comes DS to shake out a cloth or dust mop; speaks to audience) I would have been Mary all right. I didn't know you were sitting there on my patio. But since you are, don't you think I seem like a Mary? I love to meditate on ideas, especially spiritual ones. In fact, can't you just see me back in Bible days? Imagine this with me now. Me, sitting right there at Jesus' feet. Like this:

(Sits and talks to imaginary Jesus) Yes, sir, I believe that, but I never thought of it before. Would you repeat that, please, so I can get it in my notes? *(Yells)* Martha, will you stop banging the cabinet doors? I can't hear. *(To Jesus)* I see, yes. *(Whispered aside to Martha, who has come into the room)* Well, I didn't eat the last of it. Just serve something else. *(To Jesus)* Excuse

24

me, Jesus, what was that? How wonderful! *(To Martha)* Martha, for heaven's sake, will you just send Lazarus for some take-out? *(Imaginary Martha comes and whispers in her ear; she whispers back.)* Well, tell him to go by the ATM! *(To Jesus)* Tell me more about this concept, Master. If we— *(Yelling)* I can't help it if they're dirty. I didn't start it because the little magnet on the front said "Clean." *(To Jesus)* She always forgets to turn over the magnet on the dishwasher that says, "Dishes are dirty"; "Dishes are clean." Now what were you saying . . .

(Rises; large sigh to audience) That would really be nice. But I've got to stop this silly daydreaming and this thinking about Jesus. You'll have to excuse me; I've got a million things to do. *(Moves US; claps hands loudly toward side of stage)* Jamie! On the double. It's time for soccer practice. *(Pantomimes mopping at breakneck speed; calls)* Lee, let's see your homework. *(To imaginary child bringing homework for her to check)* Watch out! Don't step where it's wet! Let's see. *(Still mopping while reading. Mumbles some of the figures as she reads: 6 times 7, 4 times 8, etc.)* No, nearly every one is wrong. Go back and study your times tables. *(To another child)* Karen, the cupcakes are coming out of the oven! *(Continues mopping with one hand and opens oven with the other. Takes pan out of oven.)* Get in here and ice them if you're going to the fellowship. And hurry up; I've got to have that counter space to fix dinner. *(To Karen, who is in the same room now)* The spatula is right there in the second drawer. The third one then. Oh, for heaven's sake! That does it! *(Mimes throwing mop down)* We can never find anything. We're cleaning out these drawers right *now*. I'll do these two. You take these two. Here, Jamie, we can't leave till these drawers are cleaned out. You take these two.

(Turning to audience and offering them drawers before she realizes it) And you take these two—oh, excuse me—uh— *(Stops; embarrassed)* Well, there are certain things that just have to be done and, uh, I'm doing some routine things here, really. Nothing special. I'm just, you know, taking care of necessities. But now if Jesus could, by some miracle, drop in to visit, all that would change. I mean, I would let most of this stuff go—I'd spend lots of time with Jesus. And if something really *had* to be done, why maybe He'd even help me and we would chat while we worked.

(Begins to pantomime hurried housework again) Yes sir, you pull that Bible story out of its setting, stick it in a time machine, and plop it right down in my home, and things would be a lot different. You'd see what I'm really like: Mary all the way if Jesus were *here*. *(Turns away from audience and suddenly stops as if someone in audience has spoken to her; slowly faces front)* He is? Well, I know He's here in spirit, of course. I just meant I wouldn't be so concerned about all this housework if He were here physically. I'd definitely be more concerned about spiritual things. So since Jesus is only here in spirit— *(pause; dawning realization)* Oh dear.

Mauled

Scripture Allusion: Luke 12:15; James 1:5

Topic: Trying to come to terms with Christian view of wants, needs, and finances

Cast:
MOTHER

Scene: A shopping mall

Props:
Bench
Purse
Dollar bill
Bags of clothing

Approximate Playing Time: 6 minutes

(MOTHER *approaches a bench in a crowded mall. She plops several bags down, searches in her purse, and speaks to imaginary teenage daughter.*)

MOTHER: Here, Melissa, take this dollar and go get yourself a Coke. I need to rest a minute. No, I don't want one; just get you something. (*Daughter leaves.*)

(*To herself*) I really do want one, but I hate to spend another dollar for something I don't have to have. I never meant to spend that money for lunch—food is so expensive at the mall. Being here when the doors opened, I thought we'd be home in time for a late lunch. Oh, I just wish I had stayed home. I'm so tired. So disgusted.

(*Addresses God*) Lord, I sure would appreciate it if You'd let me have this bench for a while by myself. Because I need to talk to You a few minutes or I'm going to scream. Father, I really do care how my kids look. I want to help them find nice school clothes, but I resent outfitting them for a fashion show. No, fashion show isn't the word—they're a commercial— a walking commercial for a bunch of overpriced labels. And I really resent that. Why does it matter so much what they wear to school? Oh, I know they want to wear what everybody wears—but I mean, why does everybody *wear* that? And where do they get the money to *buy* that? I never thought I'd say this, but I wish the schools would go to uniforms. It would take a lot of pressure off a lot of kids.

(*She looks at imaginary people scurrying by.*) Dear God, what are all these people *buying*? I mean, I come here sometimes and buy things, too, things I need, but it's just getting to me today. I have this eerie feeling that I'm in the middle of a cattle stampede, only they're all laughing instead of mooing. People are passing me right and left with their arms full of packages. I heard one girl say, "I can't go home yet; I haven't bought anything. I refuse to leave until I've bought *something*." Is that how these places stay in business? What are people buying day after day, week after week? I see someone look at a price tag and say, "That's not bad." So I look at it and almost faint. I don't mind looking for a bargain. I don't mind looking all day and getting exhausted, as long as we eventually find something we need—something to make her happy with her self-image. But to go through all this and go home almost empty-handed . . .

What am I going to do, Lord? *(Takes clothes out of the bag and looks at them as she talks; add current brand names if you wish.)* These jeans cost twice as much as we usually pay, but none of the cheaper ones fit her right and these do. And this little top we found on sale is so cute, but we haven't found a thing to match it. Should I just buy her some inexpensive things and then force her to wear them? Nothing else can go on the credit card, that's for sure. Maybe if she didn't need shoes, too, but they don't make cheap shoes in triple-A width.

God, I don't know what to do. Doesn't anybody else have this problem? I just don't understand it. Jim works as hard as anybody . . . He's beginning to look so tired. *(This really bothers her; she is close to tears.)* I have to work—always wanted to stay home with the kids. Tithing, priorities, budgets—we've done it all, but it's no use—we can't make ends meet. It's not fair. *(She cries; continues talking through her sniffles.)* What ever happened to "Take no thought for what you will wear"? My only day off—need to be home cleaning the house. I don't have time for this!

(Begins moving from tears to more rational thoughts.) I should be ashamed. You know my heart, Lord. I don't ask to be rich, but I know I am, compared to lots of people. But You've placed us in this part of society where we're expected—no. No. I won't blame You for this—this stress we call society: Be happy! Get more! Better! Earlier! You deserve it! How could we be so stupid—base a whole lifestyle on lies? I don't want to be part of that, God. I want my family to fight that somehow with the truth. But how can Melissa impress anyone with her lifestyle if the word is out she's not "cool"? Do her friends approve of her—that's the first thing she wants to know. How do I respect that but teach her to be her own person? Her ego is as fragile as one of her tears, and just as likely to get wiped away.

Oh, Father, I don't know where to draw the line. That's why I sent Melissa for a Coke—my tears were that *(indicates with her fingers)* close and I don't want her to see me crying right here in the middle of the mall. I don't want to give the impression that a Christian has to be a dowdy martyr. I don't want her to think that being a Christian is miserable. But, to be honest, that's how I feel right now. Miserable . . . like a failure . . . like an ungrateful child . . . like I don't know anything about this abundant life You promise us. Oh, I know You probably meant that spiritually, but I have to live in the physical world too. You know, the one with aching feet and tension headaches and price tags that cut out your heart. It's hard to be spiritual when you've spent all you have being physical.

Well, You never said it would be easy. Or that I could have a Coke anytime I wanted one. I simply have to set some reasonable standard and stick to it, even when she thinks I've ruined her life. It's hard, You know? I guess it's my responsibility to set a limit. I'm the parent. But thank You for letting me act like a child for a minute and get all this off my chest. Oh, and Lord, I need some faith and some down-to-earth wisdom in a hurry. If You don't send it, I just may go bankrupt right in the middle of all this money and in front of all these Beautiful People.

Yes, I see the water fountain; I can drink that. And yes, You're right. It would have been better to ask You for the wisdom this morning before I left home. Sorry.

(Imaginary friend stops to talk.) Oh, hi, Rachel. I've been meaning to call you. Is your husband feeling better? Yes . . . uh—well, yeah, I was a little upset. I've had a bad morning. It was nice of you to notice. Oh, you bought me a Coke! *(Looks momentarily toward the ceiling in the opposite direction; then back to Rachel)* Thank you! *(Glances upward again with the slightest nod of her head, acknowledging God's surprise provision)*

Tracy

Scripture Allusion: Psalm 111:1; Luke 1:46-55; 2 Corinthians 1:3-5; Philippians 4:6-7

Topic: Miscarriage; praise in difficult circumstances

Cast:
>   TRACY—a young mother. She should have a pleasant voice and be capable of reading scripture in a warm, interesting way.

Scene: Her home

Props:
>   Bible
>   Rocking chair

Approximate Playing Time: 4 minutes

(Sits in a rocker; reads a Bible for a few seconds; then looks up)

TRACY: Luke 1. I remember the day. It became one of my favorites. They had asked me to read the scripture the next Sunday in the worship service. Me, of all people! Of course, I had said before that I'd be glad to do it anytime I was needed. People say I have a pleasant voice and I love reading scripture in a way that makes it come alive for me. But the first thing they ever asked me to read was the Magnificat, Mary's song of joy after being told that she was going to have a baby who would be God's Son.

> *(Reads)* "My soul magnifies the Lord, and my spirit rejoices in God my Savior, for he has regarded the low estate of his handmaiden. For behold, henceforth all generations will call me blessed."

They asked me to read about her happiness! Can you imagine being so insensitive? Well, maybe the one who asked didn't know. And if not, I certainly couldn't tell her. I felt as if my face would burst from trying to hold back the agony rising inside me. So, while I stared in shock, she rattled off times and arrangements and how she appreciated me helping out; and then she was gone.

I don't even remember driving home. The next thing I knew it was late afternoon and I was sitting in my rocker asking God how I could stand and read that passage when I had so recently miscarried.

> *(Reads)* "For he who is mighty has done great things for me, and holy is his name."

It would be too painful. I would break down and not be able to read. Like reading someone else's birth announcement at my baby's funeral.

> *(Reads)* "He has filled the hungry with good things, and the rich he has sent away empty."

(She closes her eyes and shakes her head at the memory.) To be one day so

expectant and so full of hope, and the next day so empty, so depressed. Not so much the first time it happened. Miscarriages are not that uncommon, and we could try again. But this time had been the fourth. Could I possibly read how the Lord exalted Mary when everything in me was crying, "It's not fair! Why are you doing this to me, God?" Stand and read it joyfully, as the woman said, not daring to look at my husband in the audience—and he too overcome to look at me? He had not wanted us to try that last time. He said he just couldn't take it if it happened again. But I had insisted. I wanted a baby so much.

I went to the phone several times that week to call the church and tell them I just couldn't do it. But I've never been good at saying no. And so Saturday found me looking through the Psalms for some sort of peace and comfort. But I came across several verses that speak about telling of God's faithfulness in the great congregation and declaring His love before the assembly and paying vows in the presence of His people. And so I began to think that if God would give me the strength to read joyfully about His Son's incarnation, it might somehow help me begin to come to terms with my grief. Reading in the great congregation, so to speak, like the Psalmist.

So I stood and read that Sunday. As an act of sheer will and faith, I read with believable pretense of happiness and humility and God's strange dealings with His people.

(Reads) "His mercy is on those who fear him from generation to generation. He has put down the mighty from their thrones, and exalted those of low degree." *(Puts the Bible aside)*

When I returned to the pew, my husband squeezed my hand and we wiped our eyes, almost ready to begin an aching acceptance. *(Rises)* Oh, you'll have to excuse me—that's my baby crying; he'll be ready to eat. Yes, my baby. You see, while I read, maybe even because I read, of Mary's wonder, God was working His wonders in me. As nearly as we can count it, though we hadn't planned it, God was even then molding in me a life that would not be torn away from us. A life I can hold in my arms. A life I can bring tomorrow and dedicate to the Lord in the sanctuary, our version of the great congregation. My soul does magnify the Lord, and my spirit rejoices in God my Savior. *(Rushing off)* Mommy's coming, Joshua!

Hester

Winner of Christians in Theatre Arts Sketch Writing Contest

Scripture Allusion: Matthew 6:19-20; Mark 14:3-8; Luke 6:38

Topic: Learning to give generously while we have the opportunity

Cast:

> HESTER—widow of Earl. Earl never finished high school. Even though she says Earl made a good living, this is relative. They are a plain, modest income family with a few luxuries they have saved for.

Scene: Hester's kitchen

Props:

> Small table
> Kitchen table and chairs
> Pound cake wrapped in clear plastic wrap
> Knife
> Two thick candy bars
> Small cutting board or tile

Approximate Playing Time: 6 minutes

(HESTER *is in her kitchen. A small table US holds a pound cake in clear plastic wrap. DS is a kitchen table and a couple of chairs. There is a knife lying in the center of the table, along with two thick candy bars. A small cutting board or tile is on the DS side of the table, near where the unseen visitor sits. HESTER has just heard a knock on the door leading into kitchen from the outside, which should be opposite side from the small table. She opens the door.*)

HESTER (*to unseen visitor*): Come in; come in. It's good to see you. My cake's all ready. Have a seat, and I'll get it. Uh, if you've got a few minutes to visit? Good. (*The seat she indicates should be on the DS side of the table so that* HESTER *is looking toward the audience when she addresses the seated visitor. She moves US and brings the cake wrapped for a bake sale.*) It was real nice of you to come by and pick it up. I hope we make a lot from the bake sale. I hope I got enough pieces out of it. I cut it as thin as I could. My son Jamie says I cut pound cake so thin that if he laid it on a book he could read through it. I hope it'll taste all right. It called for a tablespoon of vanilla extract, but I only put a few drops. Flavoring is so expensive now, and I try to make a bottle last a long time.

> Mmmm—smells good, don't it? Wish we could have a piece. Say, I

31

was just about to have a candy bar. Would you like one? OK. *(Gets candy bar and lays it on the cutting board or tile at front edge of the table, as if putting it there for the visitor, but in less time than anyone could pick it up, she grabs the knife, cuts it in four pieces [cuts through the wrapper], and offers one piece to the visitor/audience.)* Here you are. *(Suddenly looks at it strangely and covers her mouth in embarrassment.)* Oh, I'm sorry; how silly of me. Here, have the whole thing. Go on. *(But she continues to hold out only the one-quarter piece.)* Oh—uh—*(realizing this reveals her reluctance)* here, please. *(Places other three pieces with the first.)* Well, all right, if you're sure. *(Puts candy back on the table. There is an uneasy pause.)*

It's something I'm trying to get over, you know. Being so . . . uh . . . thrifty. Why, a few months ago I wouldn't never have donated a cake to nobody. What if I needed the sugar for my family? Or the milk for Beth? She's just a toddler. We have plenty right now, of course, but you never know what could hap—there I go again. Sorry. It's just so hard to change when I've been this way so long. And the trouble is, I never even realized it until just—*(not ready to talk about that)* I always thought it was a good habit. A penny saved, you know. Never thought of it as selfish. I was proud of it, except when my husband and my kids started in on me. Got it from Mama, I guess. Daddy was a down-and-outer. Well, a drunk is what he was, and we never knew which week there would be money for food or anything else. So Mama always stretched everything as far as she could. Never gave anything away, but it wasn't because she was selfish. She just wanted to make sure there was enough for her kids. Sometimes there wasn't. Then she would give us her share. I remember, she would sit for hours mending or taking something she saved and making it over. Not a selfish bone in her body. So maybe I didn't get it from my mama.

If I am selfish I must have got it from Daddy. I remember how he made me do. Mama had to go to work on the third shift. That left me to fix at least two meals, and I learned quick enough to make do and skimp and not complain to Daddy. To hoard whatever I had and make it last. 'Course that was a long time ago. I married Earl and he's always—was always—a good, steady provider. We have all we need and some of what we want, but I just never got used to it. See, Mama taught me it was a grace to be frugal. Stingy, Earl called it. Oh, not at first. He started off dropping little hints and making jokes. As time went on, the remarks were a little more pointy. But I still felt I was in the right and told him he just didn't mind being wasteful. I was proud of him for making a good living and wanted him to be proud of me for looking after it. I knew we're supposed to share. Really, I've heard that in church enough times. But . . . guess I planned to wait until I got enough hoarded up for us. *(Laughs sadly)* That was one of Earl's jokes. He'd say, "You know, you have pretty good morals to be such an old hoard." *(Fighting tears)* Guess I was.

Last Christmas, his sister give him a bottle of that designer aftershave lotion. Smelled so good! I couldn't believe she spent that much money. I saw him splash it on his face, and I had a fit. Next time he shaved, I took the bottle and put a little dab on each cheek and made him spread it around. He said, "Aw, Babe, you're supposed to use a lot. We both love the smell. Lemme have it."

I told him, "I know, but it will last a lot longer this way."

"But I really like it. Can't you go all out, even for me?"

"Don't be silly, Earl," I told him. "I've give you my whole life." But I still put the lotion up.

Ain't it funny how you keep fussing about the same old things? Every time I happened to catch him using that lotion, it was pretty much like that, or worse. He aimed to just do what he wanted 'cause he thought I was wrong. I remember that day he was really laying it on when I passed by, and I jerked the bottle out of his hand. He just looked at me—didn't say a word. It was later that day when I—uh—(*difficulty telling it*) I got the call that he'd been in a wreck.

I sat by him in the hospital five days. I would beg him to open his eyes and talk to me, but . . . uh . . . The first three days he would squeeze my hand when I asked, and I would pray and cry and sit some more, but his expression never changed. The fifth day I thought of it. And I went tearing home and I brought that bottle of aftershave and I said, "Here, Baby; here, Baby. You like this. Smell this, Honey." And I splashed it in my hands and rubbed it on his face. (*Crying, losing control*) And I . . . I poured the rest of it over his head and I wiped it down his hair and neck and laid my head beside his on that wet pillow. He still didn't move or speak; but as I lifted my head by his face, he smiled! I thought, "Oh, this is a good sign; he smiled." And then (*voice breaking*) he was gone. (*Pause to gain some measure of control*) And so I try to remember that some things ain't meant to always be saved . . . uh . . . might not get . . . a chance to uh . . . so . . . uh . . . and well, here's my cake. I'll try to bake two next time. (*She holds out the cake; then pulls it back and lays three of the candy bar pieces on top and offers it again.*)

Eggs in the Nest of Infinity

Scripture Allusion: Proverbs 31:30; Romans 6:5; Romans 8:18-23; 2 Corinthians 5:1

Topic: On Easter, a poetic celebration of woman: her fall from and return to grace

Cast:
ADULT FEMALE

Scene: Any

Props:
You might use a few colored eggs in some way for stage business, but don't have them in a basket with plastic grass. Instead, use a nest shape of natural materials.

Costume: Something feminine, colorful, with some ruffles

Approximate Playing Time: 3 minutes

On this day of new life,
of Easter effervescence,
I exult in my essence.
I am woman. Wonderful woman.
I awoke in the nest of Eden, daughter of the Dawning,
free to explore, adore, as I chose.
My heart embraced Adam, my mate,
but my soul sped straight toward God—
blazing, benevolent, perfect Source.
Straight, sweetly straight, was the path to His warmth,
smooth and clear of deceptive curves,
innocent of foliage for hiding;
and straightforward was my soul in its course.
Till, on a dare, I bent the path to explore
and fell through the Serpent's lair;
fell bruised and cracked down a crooked path;
down and deeper down
to a world where every soul arrives crooked,
where all creation is bent,
and God, like the sun, is still warm in intent but
hides and disappears at will.
And so do I—a small stained egg
in the thick and tempting foliage.
I strive to adapt,
for my bent is still rapt toward beauty.

Lest nostalgia overwhelm me,
I choose to view this realm as ruffled:
Ruffles are crookedness striving for beauty;
ruffles are bentness seeking perfection.
On this high holy day, where I brood with kindred souls
like eggs in the nest of infinity,
Time ruffles up toward Eternity:
There are ruffled green leaves on the deep purple violet
hiding an orange Easter egg,
and ruffled pink panties on the toddler stooping to search it out.
Ruffled teal sleeves dance on Mother's arm
as the empty basket swings on it.
Saffron wrinkles ruffle Grandmother's skin
as she grins from her seat in the shade.
And Time ruffles up toward Eternity:
Past the old broken swing with fray-ruffled rope plumed to a sturdy limb
and higher up the faithful tree
where red ruffled petals bloom, beguiling as memory's bonnet.
Higher still soar ruffled white clouds in bird-egg-blue sky
hiding great-grandmothers gone on before.
While straight, straight,
straight overhead,
faithful beyond any ruffling,
blazes in beckoning burn
the smooth, perfect, golden yolk of sun.
      Resurrection.
         Ascension.
            Return.

Alone in the Crowd

Scripture Allusion: Mark 5:24-33; Philippians 2:1-4

Topic: A woman feels isolated and not cared for, even after years in the same church.

Cast:

WOMAN

Scene: Worship service

Note: This is a modern parallel of Mark 5:24-33. It can be used in conjunction with that scripture, if desired. In any case, follow with a sermon or Bible study that addresses the topic.

Approximate Playing Time: 1 minute

WOMAN: Here I am, back in church again this week, and I'm supposed to be all joyful and excited, part of God's big, happy family. Supposed to be living a meaningful life, fulfilled in my career, enjoying close relationships with many different people. But here's how it really is. If I were to die tomorrow, nobody would even know it. Oh, I mean, they'd know it, but it's not like anybody would care. Seven years I've been at my job. A thousand people there, I guess, but it's like one big Xerox machine. Punch my ID card in the lock and here come the photocopies: "Good morning," "Good morning," "Good morning;" "Have a nice day," "Have a nice day," "Have a nice day." I don't need a nice day. I need somebody to say, "Hey, you did a great job." I'd like somebody to listen to my opinion. I'd like somebody to think I'm worth a raise. I'd like somebody to remember my name.

It's not like it's much better at church. Twelve years I've been here, but it seems like I'm always just on the fringe of belonging. I've visited this group or that, but I just didn't seem to fit anywhere. I'm here most every Sunday, give offerings, always bring something for the mission project boxes and dessert for fellowships. I've tried to set up lunches or shopping with several people—even offered to babysit, but nobody ever follows through. To tell the truth, I don't know what the problem is. I've tried everything I know. Always in this big crowd, but I'm so lonely I could die. I wish I had just one real friend. But it's just "Praise the Lord," "Praise the Lord," "Praise the Lord." "Praying for you," "Praying for you," "Praying for you"—photocopies again. They just keep on shooting out of that big, impersonal motor. Sometimes I'd like to reach out and pry open that machine and see what's really inside. But it's hard to put your hand where you know it's going to be burned.

Chained

Scripture Allusion: Mark 5:1-8; Philippians 3:18-21

Topic: An overcommitted woman becomes a victim of depression, drink, and drugs

Cast:
WOMAN—addicted

Scene: Worship Service

Props:
Bottle of pills

Note: This is a modern parallel of Mark 5:1-8. It can be used in conjunction with that scripture, if desired. In any case, follow with a sermon or Bible study that addresses the topic.

Approximate Playing Time: 2 minutes

(The WOMAN *is dressed for church but somewhat disheveled and unhealthy looking. Nervous, as if haunted by voices and afraid. If desired, she can finger the pill bottle throughout. Otherwise, she brings it out of a pocket where indicated.)*

WOMAN: What do you want with me, Jesus? Why don't you just leave me alone? I can't ever be like I used to be! *(Speaking to herself)* This is driving me crazy. Why do I keep coming here, smiling and pretending and acting like a fine Christian woman? *(Squeezes her eyes shut as if trying to shut out a voice)* Oh, be quiet! *(Opens eyes)* If I could just talk to somebody— *(looks around at audience)* but none of them would understand. Just look at them. They're really happy, not faking it like I am. They've got it all together— not messed up like me. Sometimes I'd like to scream, "How can you be so perfect? Don't you ever have doubts, make mistakes you can't fix?" But what good would that do? Nobody cares.

    I just can't take it anymore. I don't know what to believe. There are too many voices in my head. They never let up, never give me any peace. If I would just . . . just end it all, then I wouldn't have to deal with it. I could cut my wrists and then— *(Pause; weird laughter)* You know what's funny? I used to feel chained to church. This meeting, that committee; this position, that project; this program, that study course. It seemed like they wanted too much of my time. At least too much if I wanted to have time to really get ahead in my career. And I thought I was bound up in too many rules at church.

    OK, I admit, it was stupid. I really didn't realize how dangerous it was when I began to slip a little. Skipping worship service to work when I didn't have to. Giving up responsibilities at church so I could earn a little more. A social drink—for acceptance. It was all so gradual that it seemed sensible, even necessary for a modern woman. A shady deal—for a promotion. Sleeping pills for restless nights. Prozac for the stress. X-rated movies with colleagues on business trips, which led to other things.

Then I began to wonder if what my mind said was right. As soon as I decided it was, something else seemed to say how stupid I was. Finally, I couldn't trust myself to make any decisions at all. But I've still got to make them, you see, so I'm always living on the razor's edge. Depression, the doctor says. The voices say, "No way; not you." More pills.

So now all kinds of things have me in chains. Only I can't seem to break them as easily as I broke my principles. I want to, *(becomes increasingly agitated)* but they won't give me up—torment me day and night. And now, God is—I know You're there, God. *(Next sentence is not a plea, but defiant.)* Do You hear me? I know You're there, still watching me. *(Back to more pitiful, almost cringing)* Oh no, don't look at me. *(Begins to fumble with the lid to the pill bottle)* You see through it all like I was naked. God, please! I just want to go to some deserted place where I don't have to explain, don't have to lie. Take these and I'd have the courage to run my car off a cliff if I want to, and nobody would try to stop me. *(By the last word she has the lid off but is so nervous in trying to get some out that she drops the bottle so that the pills spill on the stage or steps. She runs out as if chased by an unseen force. Leave the pills throughout the service as a visual. Obviously, make sure they are fake.)*

Topical Guide

Oh My Joyce!	God's name in vain; Husband/wife relationship; Second marriage; Personhood, worth of
That's What I Want	Husband/wife relationship; Personal relationship with God
Service du Jour	Servanthood; Humor; Worship
Family Secrets	Physical abuse; Church, overlooking sin or Sin, church overlooking; Evil, confronting
Prissy Kate	Aging parents; Caregiving; Mother/daughter closeness
Found: God's Will	God's will, fear of; God's will, assumptions; Indecision
Six Flags over Church	Worship, appreciation of; Church, enthusiasm for
Mary Martha	Busyness vs. relationship; Personal time with God
Mauled	Needs vs. wants; Financial stress; Adult perspective on youth peer pressure
Tracy	Miscarriage; Praise in difficult circumstances
Hester	Generous giving; Death
Eggs in the Nest of Infinity	Womanhood; Easter; Return to God
Alone in the Crowd	Loneliness; Church, discontentment with
Chained	Addictions; Overcommitment; Backsliding

Scripture Allusions

Oh My Joyce!	Exodus 20:7; Isaiah 42:8; Romans 14:19
That's What I Want	Isaiah 30:18; Ephesians 5:28; Revelation 2:4
Service du Jour	Psalm 84:10-11; Galatians 5:13
Family Secrets	Psalm 18:46-48; Ephesians 5:28-33
Prissy Kate	Leviticus 19:32; Isaiah 46:4
Found: God's Will	Daniel 4:35; Matthew 10:38-39; James 4:14-15
Six Flags over Church	Psalm 84:1-2, 10; Psalm 100:4; Psalm 111:1
Mary Martha	Luke 10:38-42
Mauled	Luke 12:15; James 1:5
Tracy	Psalm 111:1; Luke 1:46-55; 2 Corinthians 1:3-5; Philippians 4:6-7
Hester	Matthew 6:19-20; Mark 14:3-8; Luke 6:38
Eggs in the Nest of Infinity	Proverbs 31:30; Romans 6:5; Romans 8:18-23; 2 Corinthians 5:1
Alone in the Crowd	Mark 5:24-33; Philippians 2:1-4
Chained	Mark 5:1-8; Philippians 3:18-21